GIANTS

REBECCA STEFOFF

Cavendish
Square

New York

Bags of gold and silver Jack took
    home, but still his mind did lean
Towards another prize, and journey
    up the lucky stalk of bean.
Hidden in his usual corner in the
    giant's house, he spied,
Bought for that great man's amuse-
    ment, playing sweetly by his side
While he slept, a golden harp, which
    Jack at once caught up, and ran,
But the harp with human voice cried,
    "Master, master, stop this man!"
But so tipsy was the giant, though
    he tried to run and bawl,
That, with all his pains, he could not
    stop the flight of Jack at all.

CREATURES OF FANTASY
GIANTS

BY

REBECCA STEFOFF

CAVENDISH SQUARE PUBLISHING · NEW YORK

Published in 2016 by Cavendish Square Publishing, LLC
243 5th Avenue, Suite 136, New York, NY 10016

CPSIA Compliance Information: Batch #WS15CSQ

All websites were available and accurate when this book was sent to press.

Library of Congress Cataloging-in-Publication Data

Stefoff, Rebecca.
Giants / by Rebecca Stefoff.
p. cm. — (Creatures of fantasy)
Includes index.
ISBN 978-1-50260-502-3 (hardcover) ISBN 978-1-50260-503-0 (ebook)
I. Giants — Juvenile literature. 2. Giants — Mythology — Juvenile literature. 3. Giants — Folklore.
I. Stefoff, Rebecca, 1951-. II. Title.
GR560.S74 2016
398.45—d23

Editorial Director: David McNamara
Editor: Kristen Susienka
Copy Editor: Rebecca Rohan
Art Director: Jeffrey Talbot
Designer: Joseph Macri
Senior Production Manager: Jennifer Ryder-Talbot
Production Editor: Renni Johnson
Photo Research: J8 Media

CONTENTS

INTRODUCTION

The giant Polyphemus sits atop a mountain in a 1649 painting by Nicholas Poussin.

Since the first humans walked Earth, myths and legends have engaged minds and inspired imaginations. Ancient civilizations used stories to explain phenomena in the world around them: the weather, tides, and natural disasters. As different cultures evolved, so too did their stories. From their traditions and observations emerged creatures with powerful abilities, mythical intrigue, and their own origins. Sometimes, different cultures encouraged various manifestations of the same creature. At other times, these creatures and cultures morphed into entirely new beings with greater powers than their predecessors.

Today, societies still celebrate the folklore of their ancestors—in films such as *The Hobbit, Maleficent,* and *X-Men*; and in stories such as *Harry Potter* and *The Lightning Thief.* Some even believe these creatures truly existed, and continue to walk the earth as living creatures. Others resign these beings to myth.

In the Creatures of Fantasy series, we celebrate captivating stories of the past from all around the world. Each book focuses on creatures both familiar and unknown: the cunning leprechaun, the valorous Pegasus, the cursed werewolf, and the towering giant. Their various incarnations throughout history are brought to life. All have their own origins, their own legends, and their own influences on the imagination today. Each story adds a new perspective to the human experience, and encourages people to revisit tales of the past in order to understand their presence in the modern age.

THIS IS GOING TO BE HUGE.

LAND OF GIANTS

LAND-OF-GIANTS.COM

The miniseries *Land of Giants*, to be released in 2016, is a tale of adventure and mystery in a world ruled by giants.

A BOY, A BEAN, AND A GIANT

"Fee-fi-fo-fum,
I smell the blood of an Englishman,
Be he alive, or be he dead,
I'll have his bones to grind my bread."
"Jack and the Beanstalk," recorded by Joseph Jacobs
in *English Fairy Tales*, 1890

GIANTS OF FANTASY GENERALLY LOOK like people, and many of them talk like people, but they are much larger—and much more dangerous. Chances are good that one of the first giants you heard about was in a story called "Jack and the Beanstalk," a **folktale** from England. The oldest known written version appeared in 1807, but long before that time, people probably told the tale around their fireplaces. Today it appears in many books and collections of stories.

"Jack and the Beanstalk" introduces several themes that appear in many giant tales. It also shows how such a tale can change over the years, as people shape it to fit new purposes.

Opposite: Artist Arthur Rackham drew the giant of "Jack and the Beanstalk" as a skinny fellow, with a wife and house of normal size.

Jack's Story: The Basic Tale

The version of "Jack and the Beanstalk" published by Joseph Jacobs in 1890 is probably closest to the original folktale. The story pits the young hero against an **ogre**, not a giant, but ogres and giants can be much alike in **folklore**: big, strong, and hungry for human flesh.

"Jack and the Beanstalk" tells of a boy named Jack, who lives with his poor mother. Jack takes their only cow off to sell and meets a man who talks him into trading the cow for magic beans, which the man says will grow into huge plants overnight. Jack's mother, furious at his stupidity, sends him to bed. Jack wakes to find an enormous plant outside the window, reaching to the sky. He climbs it and follows a road to a "great big tall house" and a "great big tall woman." Jack asks her for something to eat.

"My man is an ogre," she warns him, "and there's nothing he likes better than boys broiled on toast." But she gives him some food and, when the ogre comes home, she hides Jack, who sees the ogre counting his gold. After the ogre falls asleep, Jack steals a bag of gold and sneaks out. He climbs down to his home, where he and his mother rejoice at their newfound wealth.

When the gold runs out, Jack climbs the beanstalk again. The same thing happens, only this time Jack sees that the ogre has a hen that lays golden eggs. Once again Jack creeps from his hiding place and makes off with the treasure.

The third time Jack climbs up to the ogre's house, he spies the creature's golden harp, which sings beautifully. But while Jack is stealing the harp it cries out, "Master! Master!" and wakes the ogre. Pursued by the enraged ogre, Jack scrambles down the beanstalk and calls to his mother to bring an axe. Just as the ogre's legs come through the clouds, Jack chops down the beanstalk. The ogre falls

Jack thinks about trading his cow for magic beans.

to Earth and dies. Jack and his mother become rich by selling the golden eggs and showing the magical harp. In time Jack "married a great princess, and they lived happily ever after."

How Jack's Story Has Changed—and Why

"Jack and the Beanstalk" illustrates themes found over and over again in stories about giants. One theme is that giants are cruel. This is not true of all fantasy giants. Later in this book you will meet giants who are allies, or even friends, of humans. But the majority of giants are deadly dangerous. Many are cannibals—eaters of human flesh—even though they are **humanoid** themselves.

Another theme is that giants can be defeated by ordinary humans. The human heroes cannot match giants in size and strength, but they make up for that being smarter or braver than the giants. Sometimes, as in the case of "Jack and the Beanstalk," the human is simply sneakier.

In its original form, "Jack and the Beanstalk" was one of many old English tales known as "Jack stories." They are about a young man who is always called Jack. Sometimes he is stupid, careless, or foolish. At other times he is lazy. In spite of these character flaws,

Nicholas Hoult played the beanstalk-climber in the 2013 film *Jack the Giant Slayer.*

Jack almost always comes out ahead at the end of the story. In some stories his triumph is due to good luck. Often, though, Jack overcomes an enemy or wins a prize through cleverness, trickery, or crime—as the beanstalk-climbing Jack did.

What does Jack actually do? He trades his cow for "magic beans." That looks like a stupid mistake, but to his surprise one bean does produce a tall stalk. Jack climbs it, goes to someone's house, begs for food, and steals the property of the house's owner—not once but three times! When the property owner chases Jack to recover his stolen treasures, Jack kills him and keeps the treasures, without a thought for the kind widow of the fallen ogre. In a sense, Jack is nothing more than a sneaky thief.

Yet the story of "Jack and the Beanstalk" changed over the years, as people wrote their own versions and added new elements. In one version that was copied many times, Jack meets a fairy who tells him that the giant killed his father. Sometimes the fairy says that the ogre or giant stole the gold, the hen, and the harp from Jack's father, so they rightfully belong to Jack. In many modern versions of the story, the ogre—now usually called a giant—has been terrorizing and stealing from the whole land.

These changes added a **moral** lesson to the story. Instead of a thief, Jack became a brave youngster who avenges his father, or reclaims his family's treasure, or frees the land from a tyrant. In other words, Jack became good. Many folktales blur the lines between "good guys" and "bad guys." But as these old stories began to be written down for children in the nineteenth century, people felt that the stories should teach that bad behavior is never rewarded and that villains never win. In addition, someone who ends up

The Tale Type Index

The scholars and students of folktales are called **folklorists**. To compare the thousands of folktales in the world, folklorists use a tool called the Aarne-Thompson Tale Type Index that organizes the stories into groups. For example, one group is made up of "Animal Tales." Subgroups of "Animal Tales" include "the clever fox or other animal" and "wild animals and humans."

"Jack and the Beanstalk" belongs to a large group of fairy tales called "Supernatural Opponents." In these stories, human characters confront nonhuman enemies: not just giants, but also dragons, mermaids, ghosts, and other fantasy creatures.

One subgroup in the "Supernatural Opponents" category is "the treasures of the giant." In the Aarne-Thompson system, this is tale type 328. It includes "Jack and the Beanstalk" as well as the French story "How the Dragon Was Tricked," in which a clever young rascal steals a dragon's flying horse, then the dragon's bedcoverings, and finally the dragon itself. Another type-328 tale, the Italian story "Thirteenth," tells of a boy—the youngest of thirteen children—who is in danger of being eaten by an ogre. In the end, the boy tricks the monster out of its treasures, captures the ogre, and gives his captive to the king, who rewards him well.

with treasure and a princess cannot simply be a clever or tricky lad, much less a criminal. He must be a true hero.

One modern storyteller turned the traditional view of Jack and the giant on its head. In Brian Henson's 2001 television miniseries *Jack and the Beanstalk: The Real Story*, the main character is descended from Jack. The story reveals that the original Jack was a heartless thief, while the original giant was kind. The gentle, misunderstood giant is less common than the cruel monster, but it occurs in a few **myths** and in some modern stories.

2

THE UNIVERSAL GIANT

"There were giants in the earth in those days ..."
GENESIS 6:4 (KING JAMES VERSION)

GIANTS HAVE TOWERED IN THE HUMAN imagination for thousands of years. Some of the oldest giant lore comes from the ancient books or stories that formed the basis of religions. Enormous humanoids are also found in **epics**, the long poems that celebrate the history and heroes of a people or a country, and in the myths, legends, or tales of many cultures around the world.

Ancient Myths

The *Ramayana*, one of the main texts of the Hindu religion of India and South Asia, dates in its earliest form from the fourth or fifth century BCE. The *Ramayana* tells of a long war between a

Opposite: The victorious David holds the head of the slain giant Goliath.

Why Do We Call Them Giants?

The word "giant" first appeared in the English language in 1297, spelled *geant*. In 1649 an English writer named Jeremy Taylor used a slightly different spelling. He wrote, "A hundred weight to a gyant is a light burden." A few years later the playwright George Farquhar had a character declare, "I'm none of your Romantick Fools, that fight Gyants and Monsters for nothing." By 1810, when Sir Walter Scott wrote his long poem *The Lady of the Lake*, the spelling had taken on its modern form. Scott described a "Cavern, where, 'tis told, A giant made his den of old."

"Giant" comes from Greek **mythology**, which features a race of huge half-humans called the Gigantes. The Greek word *gigas* meant "giant." Over the centuries the word took on slightly different forms in the Latin and French languages, until eventually "giant" entered English. It replaced two much older English words, *ettin* and *ent*, which had meant "giant" in the languages of Northern Europe.

In the twentieth century, the English writer J. R. R. Tolkien used the old northern terms in his fantasy trilogy *The Lord of the Rings*. His invented world, Middle-earth, has a region called the Ettenmoors, a bleak home of trolls. Farther south is the land of huge walking, talking trees called Ents. As a scholar of languages, Tolkien knew that both names referred to giants.

demonic being named Ravana and the devas, or gods. Ravana's younger brother, Kumbhakarna, is a giant who spends much of his time asleep. He sleeps so soundly, in fact, that he can be wakened only after a thousand elephants have walked over him. When he wakes, his hunger is so great that he eats everything within reach, including humans.

Despite his unfortunate lapse into cannibalism, Kumbhakarna is not a bad fellow, as giants go. He is brave, loyal to his brother, and respectful of the gods, even though he fights against them as a brotherly duty. Kumbhakarna is killed by the god Rama but is said to have become part of Rama in death.

Kumbhakarna, a giant from Hindu mythology, battles a monkey army in an ancient temple carving.

Giants are mentioned in several places in the Old Testament, the part of the Bible that contains writings belonging to both the Jewish and the Christian faiths. The first book of the Old Testament, Genesis, mentions beings called *Nephilim*, a term that has often been translated from the Hebrew word meaning *giant*. The Nephilim were said to be the offspring of fallen angels who had married human women.

The Book of Enoch is a Hebrew text that dates from the first to third century BCE. Although it is not usually considered to be part of the Old Testament, it contains some of the same material. Sections 7-2 through 7-5 of the Book of Enoch tell how the half-human giants came into being after "sons of God" took wives who were "daughters of man":

And [the women] became pregnant, and they bare great giants, whose height was three thousand ells: Who consumed all the acquisitions of men. And when men could no longer sustain them, the giants turned against them and devoured mankind. And they began to sin against birds, and beasts, and reptiles, and fish, and to devour one another's flesh, and drink the blood.

These Biblical giants were portrayed not just as very tall but also as greedy, ravenous, and all-devouring. Nephilim, or giants, are mentioned later in the Old Testament as well. Some of the peoples who were enemies of the ancient Israelites, such as the Amorites, are described as giants.

The best-known biblical giant is Goliath, a mighty warrior of the Philistines, whose people are at war with the Israelites. King Saul is the tallest of the Israelites, but Goliath is much taller and fiercer. Goliath challenges the Israelites to send a champion to battle him in single combat, but neither Saul nor any of his warriors will take the challenge. Finally a young man named David offers to fight Goliath, armed only with a sling, a strip of cloth or leather used for throwing rocks. David strikes Goliath with a stone from his sling, and after the giant falls, the young hero beheads him. David, it turns out, is destined to become the king of the Israelites.

The story of David and Goliath shows how size is used in many myths and legends to represent power and ferocity. If bigger, stronger, taller men are the best human warriors, then it stands to reason that giants—bigger than any man—must be even more fearsome in battle. Only a very special hero can slay a giant. Another important part of the story is that David does not defeat Goliath by brute force in hand-to-hand combat. Instead, he defeats the giant through skill and bravery: his ability to use the sling and his willingness to step forward and meet the challenge.

Epic Adventures

Stories about giants are never just about giants. They are about how humans overcome, outwit, or tame the giants. In the *Odyssey*, an ancient Greek epic, the hero Odysseus escapes from a giant

by using his wits. The giant is Polyphemus, one of the Cyclopes (plural of **Cyclops**), a race of one-eyed giants. (The Cyclopes and other Greek giants will appear in Chapter Four of this book.)

During a long voyage home after fighting in the Trojan War, Odysseus and his men approach an island, looking for food. Book 9 of the *Odyssey* describes what they found, in the words of Odysseus:

> When we got to the land, which was not far, there, on the face of a cliff near the sea, we saw a great cave overhung with laurels. It was a station for a great many sheep and goats, and outside there was a large yard, with a high wall round it made of stones built into the ground and of trees both pine and oak. This was the abode of a huge monster who was then away from home shepherding his flocks. He would have nothing to do with other people, but led the life of an outlaw. He was a horrid creature, not like a human being at all, but resembling rather some crag that stands out boldly against the sky on the top of a high mountain.

The island is inhabited by sheep-herding Cyclopes. Polyphemus, the owner of the cave, comes home and blocks the entrance with an enormous stone. First he refuses to share his food with the men. Then the situation turns deadly:

> [W]ith a sudden clutch he gripped up two of my men at once and dashed them down upon the ground as though they had been puppies. Their brains were shed upon the ground, and the earth was wet with their blood. Then he tore them limb

from limb and supped upon them. He gobbled them up like a lion in the wilderness, flesh, bones, marrow, and entrails, without leaving anything uneaten. As for us, we wept and lifted up our hands to heaven on seeing such a horrid sight, for we did not know what else to do; but when the Cyclops had filled his huge paunch, and had washed down his meal of human flesh with a drink of neat milk, he stretched himself full length upon the ground among his sheep, and went to sleep. I was at first inclined to seize my sword, draw it, and drive it into his vitals, but I reflected that if I did we should all certainly be lost, for we should never be able to shift the stone which the monster had put in front of the door. So we stayed sobbing and sighing where we were till morning came.

The Cyclopes of Greek mythology were one-eyed giants.

The next day Polyphemus devours four more men. But Odysseus happens to have with him some strong wine and that night he offers it to Polyphemus. Once the giant is sunk in drunken slumber, Odysseus drives a sharp stake into his single eye, blinding him.

When morning comes, the blind giant must let his sheep out of the cave so they can graze. He feels each sheep's back to make sure that Odysseus and the other captives are not riding to freedom on the sheep. Clever Odysseus, though, has ordered his men to tie themselves to the sheeps' bellies. Polyphemus does not feel them, so they make their escape. They reach their boat and sail away, but Odysseus makes the mistake of boastfully shouting his name to the furious giant. He will soon regret this piece of pride, for Polyphemus is the son of Poseidon, the sea god, and he will ask his father for revenge against Odysseus.

Another man-against-giant tale comes from Cornwall, a region in southwestern England that is rich in giant folklore. Cornwall is also linked to legends about King Arthur. These may have started with a real leader of the British people against the Romans in the

Jack the Giant Killer defeated many foes with trickery rather than might.

late fifth or early sixth century, but over time they took on many elements of fantasy and magic. In 1711 an English bookseller blended the fantasy world of **Arthurian** Britain with some traditional Cornish giant tales to create a story called "Jack the Giant-Killer."

This Jack is a poor farmer's son, but he is both strong and clever. He meets and kills a staggeringly large number of giants, including a cattle-thieving giant, a two-headed giant, a three-headed giant, another two-headed giant, and many more. He spares the life of one giant, who gives Jack magical gifts, including a cloak of invisibility and a sword that can cut anything—items that Jack finds quite useful as he continues his giant-killing career. Finally Jack defeats and beheads a giant called Galligantus and frees his prisoners, including a duke's beautiful daughter. King Arthur is so pleased with the gift of Galligantus's head that he rewards Jack with a large estate and arranges for him to marry the duke's daughter.

3

LARGER THAN LIFE

"[H]e beheld a giant sitting on a huge block of timber, with a great knotted club in his hand. His eyes appeared like terrible flames of fire, his countenance was grim and ugly, and his cheeks resembled two flitches of bacon; the bristles of his beard appeared like thick rods of iron wire, and his locks of hair were like curling snakes and terrible hissing adders."

RICHARD DOYLE, *JACK THE GIANT KILLER*

A GIANT'S MOST NOTICEABLE FEATURE IS ITS size. But how large is a giant?

Oversized humanoids come in many heights. In "Jack the Giant Killer," Jack meets a giant named Cormoran, who is "at least eighteen feet high" and "so ferocious and terrible the population for miles around were kept in a constant state of consternation." The King James Bible gives the height of Goliath, the Philistine warrior slain by David, as "six cubits and a span," which would make him nearly ten feet, or three meters, tall. Compare this with the tallest known man of the early twenty-first century: Sultan Kosen of Turkey, with a height of eight feet and three inches.

Opposite: Thor, the Norse god of thunder, faces off against the enormous Skrymir.

Yet while some giants are several times the size of an average person, others are enormous. A Hawaiian folktale tells of Hana, whose ten brothers were "towering giants with bulging muscles." Hana, however, was far taller than any of them. When he was only forty days old, he was forty feet long. Eventually his great body "stretched from the mountains to the sea." In the *Odyssey*, Odysseus describes Polyphemus as towering up like a crag, or steep hill.

Besides their size, what are the characteristics of giants? Many of them act somewhat like people. They talk, wear clothing, and live in houses—although their possessions are oversized, too. Native Americans of the Pacific Northwest, for example, have tales about giant sisters called the Tah-tah Kle-Ah. In one story, the trickster Coyote changes himself into a human baby to sneak into the house of five giant sisters, where he finds that the spoons they use for eating are as big as large bowls to him.

Giants are sometimes said to be the offspring of **deities** or **demigods**. At other times they simply exist as part of the landscape of myth and folklore. In spite of much variety, there are two main types of giants. One is the crude, cruel brute that is dangerous to humans. The other type poses no threat and may even help humans.

CRUDE AND CRUEL

The threatening or monstrous kind of giant is more common than the good giant, especially in myths and older tales. These giants carry off people's livestock to eat—and who sometimes carry off people for the same reason. They may live alone or with a spouse, family, or community of other giants. Some guard hoards of treasure, as dragons do.

Cruel giants are often compared to animals because of their savagery. Polyphemus, the Cyclops, is said by Odysseus to devour men "like a lion." Some giants even have animal features, such as fangs or shaggy fur. These may live in caves and wear animal skins.

Giants may be terrifyingly strong and able to do great harm, but they are often rather stupid, or easily tricked or trapped. Jack the Giant Killer fools a two-headed giant into thinking that Jack can eat as much pudding as the giant by fastening a leather bag inside his shirt and spooning the pudding into it. Jack then tells the giant, "I can cure all wounds with a touch; I could cut off my head one minute, and the next put it again on my shoulders."

To demonstrate this miraculous power, Jack slits the leather bag with a knife. The pudding slides to the floor, leaving Jack unharmed. Believing that Jack has sliced his own belly open, the giant is "ashamed to be outdone by such a little fellow as Jack." So the giant seizes the knife, plunges it into his own stomach, and falls down dead.

TROLLS AND OGRES

Trolls and ogres are humanoid creatures similar to the cruel giant, but each has its own characteristics.

Trolls come from the legends and folklore of Northern Europe. They are linked to the earth and to a primitive way of life. They usually live in caves or mountain ranges, isolated from human society. Some trolls look almost human, or can disguise themselves as human, but most are thick-limbed, shaggy-haired, and immensely strong. Many are giant-sized. The three trolls who trap Bilbo Baggins and his dwarf comrades in J. R. R. Tolkien's *The Hobbit* are taller even than the wizard Gandalf, who tricks them into

Oversized terror stalks the far north in the 2010 Norwegian film *Trollhunter*.

arguing all night until the rays of the rising sun turn them to stone. Sunlight and lightning can petrify trolls in many folktales.

Ogres, which are always cannibals, are the darkest of these three humanoid creatures. They represent humankind's deep fears of a hostile world and the dire fates that can befall people. Ogres are usually hideous, often with colored skin, big heads, long arms, and misshapen bodies. Many are quite large. But unlike giants, who can either be cruel, neutral, or good, ogres in folklore are always savage and dangerous. The 2001 film *Shrek* and its sequels gave ogre lore a playful twist by making the green-skinned ogres Shrek and Fiona kind, smart, and not at all cannibalistic.

The Good Giant

Not all giants in legend and lore are monsters. Some are morally neutral—neither especially bad nor especially good. Others are friends, helpers, or champions of humans.

The Giant's Causeway

Were these stepping-stones made by a giant, or by geology?

Many landscape features are said to be related to giants. One of the most famous is the Giant's Causeway in Northern Ireland. It looks like a series of enormous, six-sided stepping stones leading from the coastal cliffs out into the water to disappear beneath the waves of the Irish Sea.

A causeway is a road or path through a body of water. According to legend, an Irish giant named Finn McCool built the Giant's Causeway across the Irish Sea to Scotland so that he could fight a Scottish giant named Benandonner.

The "stepping stones" are actually the remains of a large lava flow between fifty and sixty million years ago. As the lava cooled and turned into a hard rock called basalt, it cracked into tall columns, most of them with six sides. These basalt columns exist in many places around the world where lava once flowed across the land. In fact, on the other side of the Irish Sea, a cave on the Scottish island of Staffa has columns like those of the Giant's Causeway. They were created by the same lava flow that created the Causeway—or, if you prefer the legend, built by the same giant.

The mythology of Wales, in western Britain, tells of Bran the Blessed, a great king of Britain who was also a giant. Struck down in battle in Ireland, Bran told his followers to cut off his head (a common theme in giant stories) and bury it in Britain, where it would protect the land. Legend says Bran's head is buried below the Tower of London.

In Ireland, Finn McCool (Fionn mac Cumhaill in the Old Irish language) started his mythological career as a warrior, hunter, poet, and all-around hero. Over time and many retellings he became a giant as well. Said to be the son of an Irish chieftain and a woman of the fairy folk, he possessed magical wisdom that helped him defend his people. Just as Bran's protective head is buried under London, Finn McCool sleeps with his warriors in a cave beneath Ireland, from which they will emerge when desperately needed.

A postcard from the 1930s shows Paul Bunyan and his great blue ox. In the earliest stories, though, Paul was no giant.

America has its own good giant: the lumberjack Paul Bunyan, with his huge animal companion Babe, the Blue Ox. Tales about Paul's great size and strength came out of the logging camps of Minnesota and Wisconsin around the beginning of the twentieth century. They were first published as part of a lumber company's publicity campaign in 1916.

Folklorists debate whether Paul Bunyan is true folklore or "fakelore." The stories seem to have been around for a few decades before being written down, but at first they were about a lumberjack who was simply unusually large, strong, and skillful. Stories about him were tall tales about impossible feats, such as cutting down a whole forest in a day. The advertising man who collected the Bunyan stories into a booklet turned Paul into a giant.

Because giants are so much like humans, they can represent human nature and behavior at its worst and its best, its cruelest and its most heroic. To truly understand the meaning of giants, though, we turn to the most basic giant story of all: the myth of those who came before.

4

THEY WERE HERE FIRST

"The Giants, the fourth race of monsters, sprang up from his blood."
EDITH HAMILTON, *MYTHOLOGY: TIMELESS TALES OF GODS AND HEROES*

THE MYTHS OF MANY CULTURES SAY THAT before human beings came into existence the world was populated by giants. The giants had to disappear—or be overthrown and eliminated—to clear the way for a new order, one in which the human race and its gods would rule the planet.

Why do so many cultures share the myth of giants who once ruled the earth? One idea is that the story of giants giving way to humans represents the universal experience of growing up. Giants are adults as they look to children: big, loud, and in charge of everything. As the child grows up, the giants of the older generation become less large and powerful, until in time the younger generation takes over. Children become the new adults, only to be replaced by

Opposite: Mt. Etna, on the Italian island of Sicily, shakes, smokes, and spews fire—events once thought to be caused by a restless giant underground.

their own offspring. Another idea is that the vanished giants of the past stand for the crude, primitive life of people that gave way to cities and culture. The defeat of the old giants represents the triumph of civilization over savagery.

Greek mythology contains one of the best-known stories of the overthrow of giants who were here first. It is the tale of a bloody family conflict called the **Gigantomachy** (*Gigantomachia* in Greek), or war against the giants. The oldest known account of it is a work called *Theogony* (Birth of the Gods) by the Greek poet Hesiod, who lived around 700 BCE.

Titans and Giants

The Titan Kronos devours his children. Reborn, they will fight giants.

The grim story begins with the mating of Gaia, the earth goddess, and the sky god Uranus. From their union Gaia bore a series of children: first, three creatures with fifty heads and a hundred hands each, then three huge, one-eyed Cyclopes, and finally twelve enormous gods and goddesses known as the **Titans**.

As scholar Edith Hamilton says in her 1942 book Mythology: *Timeless Tales of Gods and Heroes,* Uranus was "a very poor father." He imprisoned the Hundred-Armed monsters and the Cyclopes inside Gaia. To end her pain and free her children, she gave a weapon to Kronos, one of her Titan sons. He struck his father a terrible blow. From the drops of blood that fell onto Gaia were born the Gigantes, "gleaming in their armor, holding long spears in their hands." Hesiod says that the Gigantes were strong and fierce, but does not say that they were gigantic in size.

Later writers did, however, and so they became the source of the word "giant."

Kronos (also known as Saturn) turned out to be as bad as Uranus. He imprisoned his siblings, the Hundred-Armed creatures and the Cyclopes, in Tartarus, the Greek underworld. He did not imprison his offspring, however—he swallowed them. Kronos's wife, Rhea, managed to save one of their sons, Zeus. Once he had grown, Zeus forced his father to vomit up the children he had swallowed. Zeus and his sisters and brothers then fought a war called the Titanomachy against Kronos and the other Titans. Zeus and his siblings—Poseidon, Ares, Athena, and others—won that war. They became the deities who lived on Mount Olympus, the gods and goddesses of the ancient Greeks. Then these deities plunged into a second war, the Gigantomachy. The reason for the war between the giants and the Olympian deities is not clear, but the Greeks portrayed the conflict in many works of art.

The Olympian gods defeated the giants, partly because the half-human hero Heracles (Hercules) joined the fight on the side of the gods. His particular opponent was a giant named Alcyoneus, one of the most powerful giants. Since Alcyoneus could not be defeated on his native soil, Heracles was only able to overcome him when—on a tip from the goddess Athena—he dragged Alcyoneus into another country. Together with Zeus, Heracles also defeated the giants' other great warrior, Porphyrion, who was so strong that he threatened to pull the Greek island of Delos out of the ocean and hurl it at the heavens.

After the Olympian gods won the Gigantomachy, they pitched the defeated giants down to Tartarus. Hesiod describes the fall to this dark underworld:

They sent them beneath the broad-wayed earth and bound
    them in bitter bonds . . .
[A]s far beneath the earth as Uranus is above Gaia,
so far from earth to murky Tartarus.
For nine days and nights a bronze anvil
that was going down from Uranus,
would arrive at Gaia on the tenth.
For nine days and nine nights a bronze anvil
that was going down from Gaia,
would arrive at Tartarus on the tenth.
A bronze wall runs around Tartarus.
Around its neck night in three rows is spread.

Not all of the giants were sent to Tartarus. One of them, Enceladus, was buried on the island of Sicily, near Italy. The eruptions of the island's great volcano, Etna, were said to be his breath. When he rolled restlessly from side to side, earthquakes shook the island.

In this ancient Greek carving, the god Zeus (right) battles the not-too-huge giant Porphyrion (second from left).

Bulgarian Giants and the Dreaded Blackberry

In the legends and folktales of Bulgaria, in Eastern Europe, the giants who populated the earth before humans were called *ispolini*. Yet the ispolini were not the first inhabitants of the world. First God created dwarves—their bodies smaller than humans. The dwarves were too small to fight off wild animals or to farm and build, so they died out. God tried a second time and made taller beings, the ispolini.

An ispolini could be ten feet tall or much, much taller. Some stories said that the ispolini had just one eye, like the Greek Cyclopes, or just one leg and foot. Often they possessed magical or supernatural powers. They lived in caves, fought dragons, and had such loud voices that they could call out to one another across great distances. Yet the ispolini had one great weakness: they were terrified of blackberry bushes, which they feared would entangle their feet, trap them, and cause them to starve to death.

Eventually God decided that the ispolini, like the dwarves, were not the ideal creatures to inhabit the world. He made them disappear and replaced them with humankind. Traces of the giants remain in piles of stones or old ruined buildings, which legend says are the burial grounds of the ancient ispolini.

The Giants of the North

War between gods and giants also raged in the mythology of the Norse people of Scandinavia. Yet the Norse gods and giants also intermarried or became allies at times. Odin, the father and leader of the Norse deities, was descended from Ymir, the ancestor of all the giants. Among the other Norse deities were Thor, god of thunder and

Loki, the trickster child of giants among the Norse gods, suffers for his crimes.

lightning; Idun or Iduna, who gave the gift of immortality; and Freyr, god of health and abundant harvests. The trickster Loki lived among the gods in their home Asgard but was the son of giants.

The Norse giants were called the Jotun, and their home was Jotunheim. Not all of them were larger than the gods, but some were especially huge. Among the largest were the frost giants, mountain giants, and fire giants. One of the biggest giants was Skrymir, whom Thor met while adventuring. Henry Wysham Lanier's version of the tale describes Skrymir:

There, stretched out on the ground, was a monstrous creature, so huge that he looked like the fallen trunk of some primeval fir tree. He was fast asleep, and it was his snoring which had sounded like a howling winter gale.

Many a giant as Thor had seen and encountered, the bulk of this man-mountain made him pause in astonishment. Then he quietly girded about him the belt of strength, for if ever he needed to double his powers it was now.

Just then the giant opened his eyes, which looked like muddy lakes. He yawned, stretched himself, and stood up— and his head was almost lost in the tops of the trees.

For the only time in his history Thor hesitated to join in open battle.

Thor's magic belt, which doubles his strength, is not enough to defeat Skrymir, who uses trickery and illusions to embarrass the god of thunder.

Most of what we know about the Norse gods and the Jotun comes from several books called *Eddas*, collections of Norse mythology dating from the age of the Vikings in the ninth century CE or earlier. According to the *Eddas*, the Norse gods lived with a prophecy of doom. It was foretold that Asgard would someday fall to the giants, led by a fire giant named Surt.

The fall of Asgard was part of Ragnarok, the destruction of the world. Yet Ragnarok also marked the birth of a new world in which both gods and humans would be reborn. In Norse mythology, as in Greek mythology, the conflict between gods and giants is older than the human race, but it prepares the world for human habitation.

The coat of arms of Iceland features four protectors of the land:
from bottom left, a bull, an eagle, a dragon, and a rock-giant.

PEOPLE AND GIANTS

"First [giants] made the gods tremble; then they were slain by demigods and heroes; next they became a measure of the prowess of every knight of chivalry; presently they were the sport of the childish Jack the Giant-Killer ... Besides the inconvenience of being a giant—just think of the difficulty of getting enough to eat and clothes to wear—what a disgrace to have one's head inevitably cut off by some little whipper-snapper up to one's waist or knees. And then to be such a byword for stupidity."

HENRY WYSHAM LANIER, *A BOOK OF GIANTS: TALES OF VERY TALL MEN OF MYTH, LEGEND, HISTORY, AND SCIENCE* (1922)

THE ANCIENT GIANTS OF MYTH, LEGEND, AND folklore filled people with awe, dread, and excitement. Closer to modern times, some authors have written about giants in **satire**, a kind of literature that uses humor, fantasy, or extreme exaggeration to shine a critical light on human nature and behavior.

Two writers, one in the sixteenth century and the other in the eighteenth, wrote satirical works containing some of the most memorable giants ever created. These giants are neither gods nor monsters. They are reflections of ourselves—even though the image we see is not always flattering.

Gargantua and Pantagruel

Starting around 1532, a French doctor, scholar, and monk named François Rabelais published five tales about a giant named Gargantua and his son, Pantagruel. Full of puns, wordplay, bawdy episodes, and colorful insults, these tales were grouped together under various titles, such as *The Life of Gargantua and Pantagruel*.

It takes a crowd of servants to feed the greedy Pantagruel.

Rabelais received criticism for the parts of the stories that are less than delicate, and also for their mockery of social institutions such as government, religion, and school. In the second book, for example, Pantagruel and his friends defend the land from a troop of invading giants, but not by means of heroic, soldierly deeds. Instead they get the invaders drunk, set their camp on fire, and drown them by urinating on them. One of the giants is brought back to life and tells Pantagruel about conditions in hell, where sinners' punishment is having to work at bad jobs for poor pay. In the fourth book, Pantagruel visits a land called Papimany (Pope-mania), a satirical criticism of the Roman Catholic Church.

Today the tales of Rabelais are remembered for the colorful, often ridiculous characters Gargantua and Pantagruel. The size of these giants varies from scene to scene. Sometimes they are simply quite large people, still able to enter ordinary buildings and eat

COLOSSAL CREATURES

Not all giants are humanoid. Myth and fantasy are full of huge animals. Some, such as dragons, are completely imaginary. Others, including Paul Bunyan's great blue ox, are supersized versions of real animals. One category of giant beast is the *kaiju*, a Japanese word that means "strange creature." *Kaiju*—especially *daikaiju*, or giant *kaiju*—are known to the world through movies.

King Kong, the giant ape in the 1933 film of the same name and several remakes, can be considered a *kaiju*, although he was not created in Japan. The first internally known "Japanese monster movie" featuring a giant *kaiju* was *Godzilla* (1954). This tale of a huge prehistoric dinosaur-like beast, asleep under the Pacific until disturbed by the atomic bombs that fell on Japan in 1945 during World War II, spawned many sequels, imitations, and remakes.

The original 1954 *Godzilla*.

Critics have called *Godzilla* a dark satire—an exaggeration of the very real terrors of nuclear war. *Kaiju* are often portrayed as destroyers of cities and people, but not all of them are monstrously evil. In *Gamera: Guardian of the Universe* (1995), the giant flying turtle Gamera defends the human race against enormous vampire bats, and in the 2014 film *Godzilla*, the big lizard defeats huge mutant insects that are destroying San Francisco. Like humanoid giants, *kaiju* are reflections of human fears—and of the human belief that goodness is possible.

ordinary food. At other times their size is exaggerated to absurd extremes—in one chapter, Pantagruel has a whole civilization living inside his mouth.

Always, however, the giants are shown as fat, gluttonous, loud, and rude. They are an enlargement of the greediest, sloppiest, most animal-like aspects of human nature. At the same time, however, Gargantua and Pantagruel are also intelligent, studious, loyal to their friends, and fond of fun, jokes, and good company. Rabelais seems to say that human nature is a mixture of crude and noble elements. A society that pretends to have only virtues and no vices is lying, and the idea that human beings can be saintly all the time, with no weaknesses or failings, is false.

Role Reversal

In 1726 an English-Irish writer and clergyman named Jonathan Swift published a work of fiction that soon became known as *Gulliver's Travels*. It told of the travels of Lemuel Gulliver, who, in the first of four parts, is shipwrecked and washes ashore on an unknown island. He wakes to discover that he is tied to the ground:

> In a little time I felt something alive moving on my left leg, which advancing gently forward over my breast, came almost up to my chin; when, bending my eyes downwards as much as I could, I perceived it to be a human creature not six inches high, with a bow and arrow in his hands, and a quiver at his back. In the mean time, I felt at least forty more of the same kind (as I conjectured) following the first. I was in the utmost astonishment, and roared so loud, that they all ran back in a fright; and some of them, as I was afterwards told,

were hurt with the falls they got by leaping from my sides upon the ground.

Gulliver is in Lilliput. To the tiny Lilliputians, he is a clumsy, terrifying giant. Once Gulliver wins their trust, he learns that the royal court is divided into two factions, one of which wears shoes with higher heels than the other. Lilliput is also on the verge of war with another nation over whether eggs should be broken at the large end or the small end. The disputes are absurd, but readers in Swift's day would have seen them as satires on the constant conflicts

The tables are turned in Brobdingnag, where Gulliver is surrounded by giants.

between factions in the English court, between England and France, and between the Protestant and Roman Catholic churches. And when Gulliver refuses to enslave the Big-Enders for the Lilliputian Small-Enders, his refusal is a criticism of the idea that the powerful have the right to dominate the weak. The Lilliputians, in short, stand for the all-too-common pettiness and small-mindedness of human affairs.

On Gulliver's next voyage, he is abandoned on another unknown island. His notices that the grass is twenty feet high, and then he spies the first islander:

He appeared as tall as an ordinary spire steeple, and took about ten yards at every stride, as near as I could guess. I was struck with the utmost fear and astonishment, and ran to hide myself in the corn, whence I saw him at the top of the stile [steps over a fence] looking back into the next field on the right hand, and heard him call in a voice many degrees louder than a speaking-trumpet: but the noise was so high in the air, that at first I certainly thought it was thunder.

These enormous people are the Brobdingnagians. To the Brobdingnagians, Gulliver is as small as the Lilliputians were to him. During his time in Brobdingnag, he is exhibited as a freak, played with like a doll, kidnapped by a monkey, and wounded by apples falling from a tree. Yet he also experiences kindness, friendship, and good treatment. In spite of their flaws, the large-spirited Brobdingnagians have created a more just and moral society than the nations of Europe—which, when Gulliver describes them to the king, sound petty and foolish.

With Lilliput and Brobdingnag, Swift used the idea of the giant to explore issues of power, freedom, and perspective. Moral grandness or tininess depends on how a person or a society is seen by others. Those who are great and powerful one moment may be diminished and overshadowed in the next.

GIGANTIC SAVAGES.

They carried immense bows and arrows, and large headed clubs, and talked among themselves in a tone which led us to think they were deliberating about attacking us. (See Page 184.)

A 1754 drawing of the "giants" met by European explorers at the southern tip of South America.

AROUND THE WORLD

"In 1520 Ferdinand Magellan, arriving at the straits that now bear his name, reported the existence of a race of giants that lived in the interior of Tierra del Fuego. He called them the Pataghoni, after a giant in a Spanish tale of chivalry. Subsequent travelers embroidered this account; by 1767 these giants, a wild and brutal people, had grown to about three metres (ten feet) tall ... And yet, the Pataghoni existed. They called themselves the Selk'nam or Ona, and they had an average adult-male height of 178 centimetres (five feet ten inches)— giant, then, but only to sixteenth-century Spanish sailors."

ARMAND MARIE LEROI, *MUTANTS: ON GENETIC VARIETY AND THE HUMAN BODY, 2003*

CENTURIES AGO, MOST PEOPLE THOUGHT that the world was inhabited by all kinds of strange beings, wonders that lurked on the shadowy border between myth and the unknown geography of distant lands. Dragons and other fantastic things appeared in the legends and tales of many cultures. So did giants.

Giants of Asia

One of China's oldest legends tells of Xingtian, a giant who wanted to replace the highest god. He fought with the god, but lost. The god cut off Xingtian's head and buried it inside a mountain. Still the headless Xingtian kept fighting, waving his sword and refusing to give up. "The solemn and stirring spirit reflected in this story has attracted and encouraged Chinese people for a long time," say Lihui Yang and Deming An in *Handbook of Chinese Mythology* (2005). "The hero Xingtian has become a symbol for Chinese people to express their will to resist whatever pressures and difficulties they face."

Another Chinese legend recounts the adventure of Kua Fu, the leader of "mighty giants deep in the forests of the north." One year the weather was unbearably hot. Streams dried up, the ground baked, and people suffered from the heat. Kua Fu swore to catch the sun and make it behave. He ran furiously after it. The dust from his shoes became a hill, and the stones that held down the lid of his cooking pot became mountains. Kua Fu never did catch the sun. In fact, he grew so overheated from chasing it that he drank two rivers dry. On his way to drink a lake, he died. As he was dying he planted his walking stick in the ground. It turned into a forest of peach trees that gave shade and refreshing fruit to people during hot weather.

Many giant stories tell how features of the landscape were created. In Japan, giants called Daidarabotchi received credit for lakes and ponds, which were believed to have formed in their huge footsteps. These giants could lift mountains to weigh them. When they slept they looked like mountain ranges themselves.

In Korean mythology, the giant Wang Janggun is asked to help

In Japanese tradition, lakes and ponds filled the footprints of giants.

the Dragon King of the East Sea in a war against the Dragon King of the West Sea. In spite of his fear of water, Wang Janggun agrees and shoots an arrow at the West Dragon King, striking one of his golden scales. An ordinary archer could never have killed a Dragon King, but the giant is so strong that his arrow pierces the scale and slays the dragon. He marries the daughter of the East Dragon King, and their three sons become gods of war in China, Korea, and Japan.

Native American Giants

The Aztecs were a group of Native American peoples who ruled what is now central Mexico when Europeans arrived in the early sixteenth century. According to Aztec mythology, giants called the Quinametzin had populated the earth during the era of time before humans. Four giants held up the sky. Others were responsible for founding cities and for building some of the region's largest monuments, such as the pyramids of Teotihuacan, where Mexico City now stands. The giants perished for failing to show proper respect to the gods.

Far to the north, the Iroquois people told the story of a chief and his wife who went into the forest and built a wigwam so that the husband could hunt. While he was away, the wife received a

The Aztec people of Mexico built massive pyramids. Later generations believed the builders were giants.

strange visitor: a Stone Giantess, who had run off from the land of the Stone Giants to escape her murderous husband.

For several days the giantess lived with the couple, helping the wife with her chores. On the third day her violent husband showed up: "The hunter and his wife were seized with terror when a great commotion outside announced the arrival of the Stone Giant, but the firmness and courage of the giantess reassured them, and with something like calmness they awaited the monster's approach."

The giantess ran out of the wigwam, leaped on her husband and knocked him to the ground, and told the hunter to strike him on the arms and head. Once the Stone Giant was dead, the giantess and the humans parted ways. They returned to their settlement, and she went back to her home, no longer afraid.

These days, giants are not confined to ancient myths and folktales, or to centuries-old satires. The next chapter shows that they play a big part—literally—in popular culture and modern fantasy.

WERE THERE EVER REAL GIANTS?

Giants are so common in myth and folklore that some people have wondered whether they ever really existed. Over the years people have claimed to have found the bones or mummies of giants. In 1890, a French scientist named Georges Vacher de Lapouge produced three large human leg bones from a prehistoric grave. They could have belonged to someone about eleven and a half feet (three and a half meters) tall. Lapouge claimed that the bones proved that France had formerly been occupied by a race of giants. However, another expert who examined the bones said that they were the result of the disease giantism (sometimes called gigantism), which produces abnormal bone growth, among other symptoms. Lapouge, who supported theories of white European superiority, might have been drawn to the notion that Europeans were descended from a taller, and therefore somehow superior, race.

In the United States, a scattering of reports in the eighteenth, nineteenth, or early twentieth centuries told of farmers or miners unearthing remains of giants. Many such cases can be explained as hoaxes, mistakes, or examples of disease. In any event, the supposed remains are now nowhere to be found. There is no good evidence that America—or anyplace else—was ever inhabited by giants. Yet some groups of people, such as the Masai in West Africa and the Patagonians in South America, have been taller on average than other groups. Likewise, scientists know that the humans who inhabited Europe and the Middle East ten thousand years ago were taller, on average, than those of the Middle Ages. Perhaps the finding of larger-than-average bones fueled the belief in giants.

Alien Problem? Monster Solution.

DREAMWORKS

MONSTERS
VS
ALIENS

A MONSTROUS 3D EVENT MARCH 2009

IN real 3D AND IMAX 3D

THE
MODERN GIANT

"A door opened, letting out a delicious glow of firelight, and the Porter appeared. Jill bit her lips for fear she should scream. He was not a perfectly enormous giant; that is to say, he was rather taller than an apple tree but nothing like so tall as a telephone pole."

C. S. LEWIS, *THE SILVER CHAIR*

MANY PEOPLE TODAY KNOW MORE ABOUT superheroes than about ancient myths. Movies, comics, graphic novels, and video games are more common than fireside folktales. However, the modern world is not without its own giants. Big, strong humanoids can still represent, as they always have, either supersized brutality or supersized heroism. Stories about people interacting with giants—or becoming giants—will always have something to tell us about what it means to be human.

Standing Tall in the Screen

Film and television have used giants in a variety of ways. In the 1957 movie *The Incredible Shrinking Man* (based on Richard Matheson's

Opposite: In the 2009 movie *Monsters vs. Aliens*, an ordinary woman named Susan finds her true self as the giant known as Ginormica.

1956 book *The Shrinking Man*), accidents involving insect poison and radioactivity cause Scott Carey to shrink gradually from normal human size to less than an inch tall.

The movie explores the terror of a man who feels himself disappearing from his own life, a man who can no longer work or maintain relationships with other people. Everyday objects loom terrifyingly around him. In one dramatic fight scene, he uses a sewing pin to defend himself against a much larger black widow spider. The 1981 film *The Incredible Shrinking Woman* uses the same idea for comic and satirical purposes. It features a woman who becomes ever tinier because her body's chemistry has been altered by the chemicals in everyday household products.

The year 1957 also saw the release of *The Amazing Colossal Man*, another movie in which atomic radiation creates unexpected and horrifying damage. This time it turns scientist Glenn Manning into a giant. Confused and terrified, the giant goes on a rampage and is hunted down by the military. Something similar happens in *Attack of the 50-Foot Woman* (1958, remade as a TV

In movies of the 1950s, people who became larger than life were dangerous, destructive—and doomed.

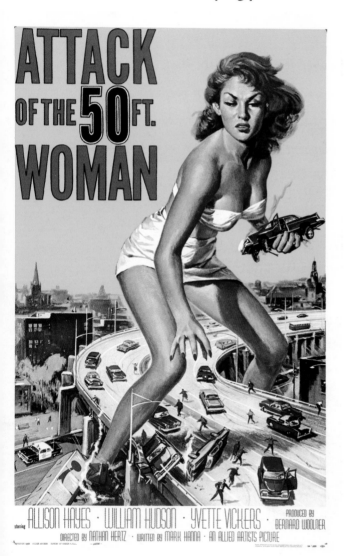

ATTACK OF THE 50 FT. WOMAN

starring ALLISON HAYES · WILLIAM HUDSON · YVETTE VICKERS · PRODUCED BY BERNARD WOOLNER
DIRECTED BY NATHAN HERTZ · WRITTEN BY MARK HANNA · AN ALLIED ARTISTS PICTURE

movie in 1993). An encounter with a UFO makes an unhappy woman, married to a rude and unfaithful husband, grow to giant size. Her anger breaks forth and she too goes on a rampage that ends only when the sheriff knocks down a power line and electrocutes her. She dies with her cheating husband in the palm of her hand.

In the 1968–1970 American television show *Land of the Giants*, a spaceship and its crewmembers are stranded on a planet where everything is twelve times larger than on Earth, the same size difference that Swift used in *Gulliver's Travels*. The crew faces constant struggles—not just hiding or escaping from the giants and their dogs and cats, but also obtaining food and the things they need to survive.

Not all giants on the screen are big trouble. In the 2009 animated film *Monsters vs. Aliens*, a woman named Susan is hit by a meteorite containing a mysterious element and turns into a giant. The government gives her the code name Ginormica and makes her part of a secret team of "monsters" that fight against deadly robots, alien invaders, and other threats. The theme of the movie is self-acceptance—at first Susan is appalled to be a monster, but she bonds with her fellow monsters and takes pride in their success, although her fiancé rejects her. Eventually she is restored to her original size, but at the climax of the movie she chooses to become Ginormica again so that she can save her friends, the monsters.

Giants also appear in various tabletop and video games. Since its origins in the mid-1970s, Dungeons & Dragons has accumulated a vast variety of giants, including fog giants, bog giants, jungle giants, and the Norse Jotun. Most are considered monsters, but in some versions of the game, players can

choose to be giants. The D&D characters called Goliaths are the descendants of giants. In the game Skyrim and other fantasy role-playing games, giants appear as dangerous opponents.

GIANTS OF MODERN FANTASY

In *Gulliver's Travels*, Swift used the plot device of role reversal. He made his character feel like a giant by surrounding him with tiny people, then made him feel tiny by surrounding him with giants. American writer Edward Eager did something similar in his 1956 children's fantasy novel *Knight's Castle*, in which four young people play with toy knights and a castle and with dolls and a dollhouse.

At night the children are magically carried into a world where the toy soldiers and dolls are larger than they are. They carry out various quests, including helping the knights defend the castle. The dolls are particularly challenging. They are bigger than the knights, so that they seem like giants when the children encounter them at night, and they want to keep the children as pets inside a dollhouse of their own.

Three years earlier, the English writer C. S. Lewis had published his own fantasy tale of children encountering giants. In *The Silver Chair*, one of the seven books of Lewis's Narnia series, two human children and their companion, a gloomy but harmless creature called a Marsh-wiggle, are sent to the magical land of Narnia to find a missing prince. Along the way they seek shelter from a snowstorm in Harfang, the city of the Gentle Giants, who feed the travelers well. The chance discovery of a cookbook reveals that the giants are not so gentle after all—they are fattening the three travelers up in order to cook them for a feast. The children escape by fleeing into a tunnel while the giant king bellows, "After them, after them, or we'll have no man-pies tomorrow."

Lewis's friend J. R. R. Tolkien used both giants and trolls in his fantasy novels. In *The Hobbit*, Bilbo Baggins and his companions are almost cooked by trolls. Afterward, while traveling in the mountains, they are in dire perils when "stone-giants" toss huge boulders around for fun. Later, Gandalf the wizard speaks of finding a "decent giant" to block up a passageway leading to a goblin lair. Giants and trolls are also mentioned in *The Lord of the Rings*, although they do not play important roles.

Giants loom larger in one of the most popular and successful fantasy creations of modern times, the series of seven novels about young wizard Harry Potter, written by J.K. Rowling. The giants of Potter's world are large but not super-colossal—they can be as much as twenty-five feet or so (eight meters) in height. Although they are intelligent, they are also typically coarse and violent. As Rubeus Hagrid, the big, crude gamekeeper at the wizard school Hogwarts, says in *Harry Potter and the Order of the*

Rubeus Hagrid, one of the most popular characters in the Harry Potter books, is the son of a giantess.

Phoenix, "They're not meant ter live together, giants ... they can't help themselves, they half kill each other every few weeks."

In Harry Potter's time, giants live in hiding in wild places. They had been driven into the wilderness by the wizards after siding with the evil Lord Voldemort in an earlier war. In the course of Harry's story, both the wizards and Lord Voldemort try to make an alliance with the giant leader, who is called the Gurg. When war comes again, most of the giants once again side with Voldemort. One giant, however, is different. He is Grawp, a rather puny giant—only sixteen feet tall, bullied by the others—who is the son of a giantess named Fridwulfa. The same giantess, it turns out, was the mother of gamekeeper Hagrid, although his father was human.

Hagrid saves his half-brother from the cruel giants and brings him to live near Hogwarts. Despite the fact that many people in the wizarding world are prejudiced against giants, Grawp fights on the side of the wizards to defend Hogwarts in Voldemort's attack.

In the Harry Potter stories, most giants are cut off from human society, partly by their own choice. Several "good" characters, however, turn out to be half-giants—including the beloved Hagrid. In Hagrid, Rowling created a character that combined the size and roughness of folktale giants with the gentleness of a loving heart. He is part of the long line of giants that stretches from ancient myths about the creation of the world to the fantasy adventures of the present day. Giants are often related to stone and mountains. Like mountains, they have endured for ages and will endure into the future.

GLOSSARY

Arthurian Having to do with the history or legend of King Arthur of Britain.

Cyclops One of the Cyclopes, a group of giants in Greek legends; each Cyclops had a single eye in the middle of its forehead.

deity A god or goddess.

demigod A being who is half-god; the offspring of a god and a mortal or a god and another supernatural being.

epic A long work (usually a poem) about the history and heroes of a particular culture or country; epics usually celebrate a people's glorious history.

folktale A story that occurs in several versions and can be traced back for a long time in one or more cultures; anyone may write down and publish a folktale, but the original author is not known.

folklore A body of stories, songs, and sayings within a culture; traditional folklore was passed from generation to generation in spoken form before being written down.

folklorist A scholar or student of folklore.

Gigantomachy War against the giants; from the Greek word *gigantomachia*.

humanoid Having the form of a human.

kaiju Japanese word for "strange creature," often a movie monster; giant monsters may be called *daikaiju*.

moral In a story, a moral is the lesson that the story is supposed to teach; it usually shows good behavior being rewarded and bad behavior being punished.

myth A story about deities or beings related to the gods; a myth that is, or once was, sacred or religious.

mythology A particular culture's body of myths: stories about deities, the origins of the world and of people, and other sacred or deeply meaningful subjects.

ogre A fantasy being that is big and strong, often with a large head and long arms, and eats humans; not all ogres are giants, and not all giants are ogres, but the two are related in folklore, and many cruel giants are similar to ogres.

satire The use of humor, fantasy, or exaggeration to criticize or make a point about human behavior and weaknesses, or about politics or public affairs.

Titan In Greek mythology, one of the supernatural beings who ruled Earth before the gods; Titans and giants have sometimes been confused for each other or combined into a single gigantic race.

troll A supernatural or legendary being from Northern European lore, sometimes giant-sized, usually hostile and associated with earth, stone, and a primitive way of life.

To Learn More About Giants

Books

Christopher, Neil. *Arctic Giants*. Iqaluit, Nunavut: Inhabit Media, 2010.

Ganeri, Anita. *Giants and Ogres*. New York: PowerKids Press, 2010.

Jeffrey, Gary, and Nick Spender. *Graphic Mythical Creatures: Giants*. New York: Gareth Stevens Publishing, 2011.

Website

Greek Giants

www.amnh.org/exhibitions/past-exhibitions/mythic-creatures/land-creatures-of -the-earth/greek-giants

The American Museum of Natural History offers an excellent overview of Greek giants and their role in mythology as part of its Mythic Creatures website.

Video

The Giant's Causeway on Video

www.ireland.com/en-gb/what-is-available/walking-and-hiking/coastal-walks /destinations/northern-ireland/county-antrim/bushmills/articles/giants -causeway-video

Watch this short video and explore the myth and the science behind the Giant's Causeway on the Irish Coast.

Bibliography

Clute, John, and John Grant, eds. *The Encyclopedia of Fantasy*. New York: St. Martin's, 1999.

Cotterell, Arthur, and Rachel Storm. *The Ultimate Encyclopedia of Mythology*. London: Anness Publishing, 1999.

Dewhurst, Richard. *The Ancient Giants Who Ruled America: The Missing Skeletons and the Great Smithsonian Cover-Up*. Rochester, VT: Bear and Company, 2014.

Goldberg, Christine. "The Composition of 'Jack and the Beanstalk.'" *Marvels & Tales: Journal of Fairy-Tale Studies* 15, no. 1 (2001): 11–26.

Hansen, William. *Classical Mythology: A Guide to the Mythical World of the Greeks and Romans*. New York: Oxford University Press, 2005.

Lanier, Henry Wysham. *A Book of Giants: Tales of Very Tall Men of Myth, Legend, History, and Science*. New York: Dutton, 1922.

Lewis, Jon E., ed. *A Brief Guide to Native American Myths and Legends*. 2nd edition. Originally published by Lewis Spence in 1914.

Lindow, John. *Norse Mythology: A Guide to Gods, Heroes, Rituals, and Beliefs*. New York: Oxford University Press, 2002.

Rose, Carol. *Giants, Monsters, and Dragons: An Encyclopedia of Folklore, Legend, and Myth*. New York: W.W. Norton, 2001.

Time-Life Books, eds. *Giants and Ogres*. Alexandria, VA: Time-Life Books, 1985.

Index

About the Author

Rebecca Stefoff grew up in the Midwest, completed graduate studies in English literature at the University of Pennsylvania, and now lives in the Pacific Northwest. She has written books for young readers on many topics in literature, history, science, and exploration. A long-time reader of fantasy, folklore, and mythology, she explored many related topics in her five-volume series *Secrets of the Supernatural* (Marshall Cavendish Benchmark, 2008). More recently, she wrote the six-volume series *Is It Science?* (Cavendish Square, 2014) and the four-volume series *Animal Behavior Revealed* (Cavendish Square, 2014). You can learn more about Stefoff and her books for young people at www.rebeccastefoff.com.